AL•LEONARD
INSTRUMENTAL
PLAY-ALONG

AUDIO
ACCESS
INCLUDED

PLAYBACK+
Speed • Pitch • Balance • Loop

TRUMPET

Disney MARY POPPINS RETURNS

MUSIC BY MARC SHAIMAN
LYRICS BY SCOTT WITTMAN AND MARC SHAIMAN

Audio Arrangements by Peter Deneff

To access audio, visit:
www.halleonard.com/mylibrary

Enter Code
2823-7737-7770-1456

ISBN 978-1-5400-4589-8

Visit Hal Leonard Online at
www.halleonard.com

Contact us:
Hal Leonard
7777 West Bluemound Road
Milwaukee, WI 53213
Email: info@halleonard.com

In Europe, contact:
Hal Leonard Europe Limited
42 Wigmore Street
Marylebone, London, W1U 2RN
Email: info@halleonardeurope.com

In Australia, contact:
Hal Leonard Australia Pty. Ltd.
4 Lentara Court
Cheltenham, Victoria, 3192 Australia
Email: info@halleonard.com.au

CAN YOU IMAGINE THAT?

TRUMPET

Music by MARC SHAIMAN
Lyrics by SCOTT WITTMAN and MARC SHAIMAN

A CONVERSATION

TRUMPET

Music by MARC SHAIMAN
Lyrics by SCOTT WITTMAN and MARC SHAIMAN

A COVER IS NOT THE BOOK

TRUMPET

Music by MARC SHAIMAN
Lyrics by SCOTT WITTMAN and MARC SHAIMAN

(Underneath the)
LOVELY LONDON SKY

TRUMPET

Music by MARC SHAIMAN
Lyrics by SCOTT WITTMAN and MARC SHAIMAN

rit.   *p*   *mf* a tempo

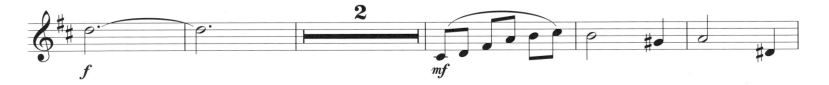

f   **2**   *mf*

rit.

f ————————— *mf*   *mp* ——— *p*

a tempo   rit.

NOWHERE TO GO BUT UP

TRUMPET

Music by MARC SHAIMAN
Lyrics by SCOTT WITTMAN and MARC SHAIMAN

THE PLACE WHERE LOST THINGS GO

TRUMPET

Music by MARC SHAIMAN
Lyrics by SCOTT WITTMAN and MARC SHAIMAN

THE ROYAL DOULTON MUSIC HALL

TRUMPET

Music by MARC SHAIMAN
Lyrics by SCOTT WITTMAN and MARC SHAIMAN

TRIP A LITTLE LIGHT FANTASTIC

Music by MARC SHAIMAN
Lyrics by SCOTT WITTMAN and MARC SHAIMAN

TRUMPET

TURNING TURTLE

TRUMPET

Music by MARC SHAIMAN
Lyrics by SCOTT WITTMAN and MARC SHAIMAN

Fast Broadway 2